THE
ELECTRIC ELEPHANT
and Other Stories

CAROLYN GRAHAM

VCC, KING EDWARD CAMPUS
ESL/VOC
1155 EAST BROADWAY
VANCOUVER, B.C.   V5T 4N3

New York   Oxford
OXFORD UNIVERSITY PRESS
1982

Oxford University Press

200 Madison Avenue
New York, N.Y. 10016 USA

Walton Street
Oxford OX2 6DP England

OXFORD is a trademark of Oxford University Press.

Library of Congress Cataloging in Publication Data

Graham, Carolyn.
   The electric elephant, and other stories.

   Summary: An intermediate reader for students of
English as a second language, featuring anecdotes,
riddles, and jokes, accompanied by exercises and
activities.
   1. English language—Text-books for foreigners.
2. Readers—1950–   [1. English language—
Textbooks for foreigners.   2. Readers.   3. Wit and
humor]   I. Mooney, Gerry, ill.   II. Title.
PE1128.G64   1982   428.6′4   82-12522
ISBN 0-19-503229-2 (pbk.)

Copyright © 1982 by Oxford University Press, Inc.

First published 1982
10 9 8 7 6 5 4 3

All rights reserved. No part of this publication may be reproduced, stored in a re-
trieval system, or transmitted, in any form or by any means, electronic, mechanical,
photocopying, recording, or otherwise, without the prior permission of Oxford University Press.

This book is sold subject to the condition that it shall not, by way of trade or otherwise,
be lent, re-sold, hired out, or otherwise circulated without the publisher's prior con-
sent in any form of binding or cover other than that in which it is published and
without a similar condition including this condition being imposed on the subsequent
purchaser.

Illustrations by Gerry Mooney

Printed in the United States of America

To George Bacon
Wherever you are

Contents

To the Teacher

The anecdotes in *The Electric Elephant* are designed for adult students of English as a Second Language at the intermediate or low-intermediate level.

The stories themselves and the jokes and riddles included in each chapter offer the students a broad sampling of American humor and provide a model for developing oral story-telling skills.

Each chapter contains a story illustrated by a drawing and accompanied by a set of exercises to provide additional practice in listening, speaking, reading, and writing. Each chapter concludes with a joke illustrated by a drawing.

THE SOURCE OF THE ANECDOTES

The origin of jokes and humorous stories is often difficult to trace, but as they are passed from one generation to another they become part of the folk history of the people. In a few cases the stories in *The Electric Elephant* were based on supposedly real events and involved historical figures such as Abraham Lincoln, Grandma Moses, and George Bernard Shaw. The story "Margie and Paul" is loosely based on a conversation that is said to have taken place between Lady Astor and Winston Churchill. "How To Meet Men" was inspired by an incident attributed to the American humorist Dorothy Parker. "Dreams" was based on a line from G. B. Shaw, and the idea for "Men and Lions" originated in Aesop's Fables.

SUGGESTIONS FOR PRESENTING THE STORIES

The teacher may wish to begin by simply telling the story in his or her own words, while the students listen with books closed. Careful explanation might be necessary to help the students appreciate the humor and have a clear understanding of the events of the story.

I have found it very helpful to give the students the vocabulary to express their response to the story, particularly if they didn't quite understand it. I make a point of teaching such expressions as "I didn't get it," "What's so funny?" "I missed the punch line," etc.

Following the initial presentation, I would have the students open their books and listen while I read the story a second time. They are then ready to move on to the first exercise.

The drawing may also be used for question practice and classroom discussion, or students may be divided into groups and asked to invent a completely new story based on the same drawing.

USING THE EXERCISES

In addition to the illustrated anecdotes, each chapter contains the following types of exercises:

A LISTEN AND COMPLETE   This is a listening comprehension exercise, focusing on the recognition of articles and prepositions. The teacher reads the complete story at normal speed while students listen with books closed. The students then open their books, and as the teacher reads the story a second time they fill in the missing words in the spaces provided. Students may check their own work by re-reading the original story.

B WHAT DO YOU THINK?   This is an exercise in reading comprehension. Students circle the BEST answer to each question. The answers may then be discussed in class. You may wish to divide the students into small groups for this and the following exercise.

C LEARNING NEW WORDS   This is an exercise in vocabulary development. Students may be divided into small groups to complete this exercise. The teacher may then wish to discuss appropriate usage, setting the words in context.

D MIX AND MATCH   In this exercise, students select any item they wish from Lists A, B, and C to form a complete sentence. There is no one correct way. Some combinations would obviously be more logical than others, but a student might decide to have fun with the words and make some more imaginative connections. You might wish to give a homework assignment in which the students create their own lists for A, B, and C. These new word lists could later be shared in class and would form the basis for a new set of sentences created by the students working in small groups.

E ASK YOUR PARTNER   In this exercise, students are divided into pairs and question each other, writing the answers in the spaces provided.

F PUT IT IN WRITING   This exercise provides the students with writing practice, using the material they have learned in E. It may be used as a homework assignment or as the basis for an oral or written composition.

HAVE YOU HEARD THIS ONE?   Each chapter ends with a simple joke or riddle, illustrated by a drawing. This exercise may be used as a guessing game by covering the answer and asking the students to study the picture and try to guess the correct response.

WHAT IS GREY, HAS FOUR LEGS,
WEIGHS 8000 POUNDS, AND LIGHTS UP IN THE DARK?

An electric elephant

1 *Bilingual Education*

One morning, a wise old mother cat was walking through the neighborhood with her two baby kittens. Suddenly they saw a huge dog standing in front of them. The kittens were terrified and in their tiny little voices cried, "Mew, mew, mew, mew." The big dog stared at them and growled, "Grrrrrrr! Grrrrrr! Grrrrrrr! Grrrrrrrr!"

The mother cat stood very still, looked him in the eye, opened her mouth, and said, "Grrrrrrrr! Grrrrrrrrrr!" The dog was astonished. "Grrrrrrrr! Grrrrr!" he answered and quickly walked away.

The mother cat smiled and turned to her kittens. "Now," she said, "I hope you understand the importance of learning a second language."

A. Listen and Complete

Listen to your teacher read the story and fill in the missing words in the spaces indicated.

_____ morning, _____ wise

_____ mother cat _____ through

_____ neighborhood _____ baby

_____ . Suddenly _____ saw

_____ dog standing _____ .

_____ kittens _____ terrified

_____ tiny little _____ cried, "Mew,

mew, mew, mew." _____ dog stared

_____ growled, "Grrrrrrrrrr! Grrrrrrr! Grrrrrrrrrr!

Grrrrrrrrr!"

    _____ mother cat stood _____ still,

looked _____ eye, opened _____ mouth,

_____ said, "Grrrrrrrrrr! Grrrrrrrrrrr!"

    _____ dog _____ astonished. "Grrrrrrrr!

Grrrrrrrrr!" _____ answered _____

walked _____ .

    _____ mother cat _____ and

_____ kittens. "Now," _____ , "I hope

_____ understand _____ importance

_____ learning _____ second language."

B. What Do You Think?

Circle the best answer to each of the following questions.

1. What did the mother cat and her kittens see when they were walking through the neighborhood?
   a) an old friend
   b) a huge dog
   c) a little puppy

2. What did the big dog do when he saw them?
   a) he laughed
   b) he growled
   c) he ran away

3. What did the old mother cat do?
   a) she pretended to be asleep
   b) she spoke to him in his own language
   c) she panicked

C. Learning New Words

Study the words below. Indicate in the spaces provided whether they are similar (S) or opposite (O) to the words in the boxes.

TERRIFIED	unafraid	_____
	scared	_____
	frightened	_____
	panicked	_____
TINY	little	_____
	wee	_____
	very small	_____
	huge	_____
HUGE	enormous	_____
	king-sized	_____
	big	_____
	miniature	_____

D. Mix and Match

Complete the following sentence in four different ways. Use any vocabulary you like from lists A, B, and C.

	A		B
When the man saw the	_____		_____
	_____		_____
	_____		_____
	_____		_____

C

he stopped suddenly and _____

_____

_____

_____

_____

A	B	C
little puppy baby kitten big angry dog tiger	running towards him watching him staring at him following him	said, "Hi, there." cried, "Help." shouted, "Get out of here." said, "Here, kitty, kitty, kitty."

E. Ask Your Partner

Ask your partner the following questions. Write the answers in the space provided.

		Yes	No
1.	Do you think English is an easy language to learn well?		
2.	Do you write English as well as you read it?		
3.	Does your father speak English?		
4.	Does your mother speak English?		
5.	Do you speak English every day outside of the classroom?		
6.	Do you usually speak English at home?		
7.	What's your native language?		
8.	How many languages do you speak?		
9.	How long have you studied English?		
10.	How long does it take to learn English well?		

F. Put It in Writing

Write ten complete sentences about your partner, using the information you have learned in Exercise E.

Example: If your partner answered **YES** to the first question, you will write:
He thinks that English is an easy language to learn well.

Have You Heard This One?

WHAT DID ONE WALL SAY TO THE OTHER?

I'll meet you at the corner.

2 Twins

Once there were two brothers who were identical twins. They looked exactly alike. They both had the same curly dark brown hair, blue eyes, and beautiful teeth. They were both exactly 5′ 10″ tall and both weighed exactly 150 pounds.

They not only looked alike but also sounded alike on the telephone. Not even their family could tell the difference. They dressed alike, listened to the same music, and read the same books. They even laughed at the same jokes.

When they were twenty-three they both got married and a year later both had sons. The years went by and as they began to grow old, they both wore glasses and eventually they both became bald.

Then one day, one of the brothers got sick and died. A few days later a man stopped the other twin on the street.

"Excuse me for asking," he said, "but was it you or your brother who died?"

A. Listen and Complete

Listen to your teacher read the story and fill in the missing words in the spaces indicated.

_____ there _____ two brothers who _____ identical twins. They looked _____ alike. They _____ had _____ curly dark brown hair, _____ eyes, and _____ teeth. They _____ both _____ 5′ 10″ tall and both _____ exactly _____ pounds.

They _____ looked alike _____ sounded alike _____ telephone. _____ family _____ tell _____ difference. They _____ alike, listened _____ music, and read _____ books. They _____ laughed _____ jokes.

When _____ twenty-three _____ got married _____ year later _____ had sons. _____ years went by _____ began to grow old, _____ wore glasses and eventually _____ both _____ bald.

Then _____ day, _____ brothers got sick and died. _____ days later a man _____ twin _____ street.

"Excuse _____ asking," _____, "but _____ or _____ brother _____ died?"

B. What Do You Think?

Circle the best answer to each of the following questions.

1. Why did people have trouble telling the two men apart?
   a) they were brothers
   b) they were the same age
   c) they were identical twins

2. Who did the men look like?
   a) they looked like each other
   b) they looked like their Uncle Harry
   c) they looked like famous movie stars

3. What was the one difference between the two men?
   a) one was shorter than the other
   b) one got married and had a son
   c) one got sick and died

C. Learning New Words

Study the words below. Indicate in the spaces provided whether they are similar (S) or opposite (O) to the words in the boxes.

IDENTICAL	exactly alike	_____
	the same as	_____
	impossible to tell apart	_____
	easy to distinguish	_____

EXACTLY	specifically	_____
	precisely	_____
	sort of	_____
	more or less	_____

EVENTUALLY	after a while	_____
	some time later	_____
	immediately	_____
	right now	_____

D. Mix and Match

Complete the following sentences in four different ways. Use any vocabulary you like from lists A, B, and C.

A

Once I had two _____ who looked exactly alike.

_____

_____

_____

B   C

They both had _____ and loved _____

_____   _____

_____   _____

_____   _____

A	B	C
friends	big brown eyes	to talk.
aunts	long black curly hair	to tell stories.
teachers	big ears	to eat cheese.
dogs	dimples	to take long walks.

E. Ask Your Partner

Ask your partner the following questions. Write the answers in the space provided.

	Yes	No
1. Are you an only child?	_____	_____
2. Are you taller than your mother?	_____	_____
3. Do you look like your father?	_____	_____
4. Have you ever met anyone who looked very much like you?	_____	_____
5. Do you and your parents enjoy the same kind of music?	_____	_____
6. Do you and your good friends laugh at the same jokes?	_____	_____
7. Have you ever met a pair of identical twins?	_____	_____
8. Would you like to have twins?	_____	_____
9. If you had twin sons, what would you call them?	_____	
10. If you had identical triplets, how would you tell them apart?	_____	

F. Put It in Writing

Write ten complete sentences about your partner, using the information you have learned in Exercise E.

Example: If your partner answered **NO** to the first question, you will write: He isn't an only child.

Have You Heard This One?

**WHAT DID THE MAN SAY TO THE OIL AND VINEGAR
WHEN HE SAW THEM ON THE KITCHEN TABLE?**

Oh, pardon me, I didn't realize you were dressing!

3 The Gorilla in Macy's

A gorilla went shopping in Macy's one day. He was in the umbrella department, on the first floor, opening and closing the umbrellas and throwing them on the floor. He seemed to be getting very angry.

A customer was watching all this and finally ran up to a clerk and said, "Excuse me, but there's an angry gorilla over there playing with the umbrellas."

"I'm sorry," said the clerk, "but that's not my department. Try the third floor." So the customer ran to the third floor, found the manager, told him the story, and they both rushed back to the gorilla. The manager was trembling, but he tried to smile and walked right up to the big beast, saying, "Pardon me, Sir or Madam but, well, you know we've never seen a gorilla in Macy's before."

"I'm not surprised," said the gorilla, "and with these prices you're not going to see many more either."

A. Listen and Complete

Listen to your teacher read the story and fill in the missing words in the spaces indicated.

_____ gorilla went shopping _____
Macy's _____ day. He was _____
umbrella department, _____ first floor, opening and closing
_____ umbrellas and throwing _____
floor. He seemed _____ getting _____
angry.

_____ customer _____ watching
_____ and finally ran _____ clerk and
said, "Excuse me, _____ angry gorilla
_____ playing _____ umbrellas."

"I'm sorry," _____ clerk, "but _____
my department. Try _____ floor." So the customer ran
_____ floor, found _____ manager, told
_____ story, and _____ rushed
_____ gorilla. _____ manager
_____ trembling, _____ tried to smile
and walked _____ big beast, saying, "Pardon me, Sir or
Madam _____, well, _____ we've
_____ seen _____ gorilla
_____ Macy's before."

"I'm _____ surprised," said the gorilla, "and with
_____ you're _____ going to see
_____ either."

B. What Do You Think?

Circle the best answer to each of the following questions.

1. Why was the customer so surprised?
   a) the prices were so high
   b) there was no manager on the first floor
   c) he saw a gorilla among the umbrellas

2. Why was the gorilla angry?
   a) the umbrellas were so ugly
   b) they didn't have an umbrella in his size
   c) the umbrellas were overpriced

3. What did the customer do when he first saw the gorilla?
   a) he went home and took an aspirin
   b) he ran to a clerk
   c) he called his psychiatrist

C. Learning New Words

Study the words below. Indicate in the spaces provided whether they are similar (S) or opposite (O) to the words in the boxes.

TO BE SURPRISED		
	to be amazed	_____
	to be astonished	_____
	to be startled	_____
	to expect	_____

TO BE VERY ANGRY		
	to be furious	_____
	to be delighted	_____
	to be mad	_____
	to be pleased	_____

TO TREMBLE		
	to shake	_____
	to quiver	_____
	to be steady	_____
	to vibrate	_____

D. Mix and Match

Complete the following sentence in four different ways. Use any vocabulary you like from lists A, B, and C.

A

One morning a woman _____

_____

_____

_____

B   C

when all of a sudden she_____   _____

_____   _____

_____   _____

_____   _____

A	B	C
was shopping	felt	something burning.
was waiting at the bus stop	saw	a funny noise.
was cooking breakfast	heard	something furry on
was walking down the	smelled	her ankle.
street		an awful sight.

E. Ask Your Partner

Ask your partner the following questions. Write the answers in the space provided.

	Yes	No
1. Have you ever worked in a department store?	_____	_____
2. Are you a careful shopper?	_____	_____
3. Do you always pay in cash?	_____	_____
4. Did you spend any money today?	_____	_____
5. Do you like large department stores better than small neighborhood shops?	_____	_____
6. Did you bring an umbrella to class today?	_____	_____
7. Is it difficult for you to find your correct size in a clothing store?	_____	_____
8. Have you ever lost an umbrella?	_____	_____
9. Do you like to go window-shopping?	_____	_____
10. Have you ever seen a gorilla?	_____	_____

F. Put It in Writing

Write ten complete sentences about your partner, using the information you have learned in Exercise E.

Example: If your partner answered **NO** to the first question, you will write:
He hasn't ever worked in a department store.

Have You Heard This One?

WHERE DOES A 400-POUND GORILLA USUALLY SLEEP?

Anywhere he wants to!

4 How To Meet Men

A very amusing and intelligent writer went to work for a large magazine in New York. She loved her job and had only one complaint: she had no opportunity to meet any of the other writers. Most of them were men, and they behaved as if they didn't know she was there.

One day she was having lunch with Ellen, an old friend who knew about her problem.

"How are things going at the office?" asked Ellen.

"Just fine," she answered.

"Have you met any interesting men?" she asked.

The writer smiled and answered, "I've met every man in the office."

"Really!" said Ellen. "How did you do it?"

"It was easy," said the writer. "I just put a sign on my office door."

"A sign?" said Ellen. "What did it say?"

"Oh," said the writer, "it was just three letters, 'M-E-N.'"

A. Listen and Complete

Listen to your teacher read the story and fill in the missing words in the spaces indicated.

_____ amusing _____ intelligent

_____ writer went _____ work

_____ large magazine _____ New York.

_____ loved _____ and

_____ one complaint: _____ no

opportunity _____ meet _____ other

writers. Most _____ were men, _____

behaved _____ didn't know _____ there.

One day she _____ lunch _____

Ellen, _____ friend _____ knew

_____ problem.

"How _____ things going _____

office?" _____ Ellen.

"_____," she answered.

"Have _____ interesting men?" she _____.

_____ writer smiled _____ answered,

"I've met _____ man _____ office."

"Really!" _____ Ellen. "How _____

you _____ it?"

"It _____ easy," said _____ writer. "I

_____ put _____ sign

_____ office door."

"_____ sign?" said Ellen. "What

_____ say?"

"Oh," _____ writer, "it _____ just

three letters, _____.' "

B. What Do You Think?

Circle the best answer to each of the following questions.

1. What was the woman complaining about?
   a) her job was too difficult
   b) her boss was unfriendly
   c) she never met any of the men in the office

2. What was her solution?
   a) she dyed her hair blond
   b) she put a sign on her office door
   c) she looked for another job

3. What did the sign say?
   a) Keep Off the Grass
   b) In Case of Fire, Do Not Use the Elevator
   c) M-E-N

C. Learning New Words

Study the words below. Indicate in the spaces provided whether they are similar (S) or opposite (O) to the words in the boxes.

AMUSING		
	funny	_____
	humorless	_____
	humorous	_____
	serious	_____

INTELLIGENT		
	dumb	_____
	bright	_____
	smart	_____
	sharp	_____

TO COMPLAIN		
	to gripe	_____
	to whine	_____
	to grumble	_____
	to compliment	_____

D. Mix and Match

Complete the following sentence in four different ways. Use any vocabulary you like from lists A, B, and C.

A

A very _____ woman got an excellent job, but she

_____

_____

_____

B   C

_____ it because her boss was _____

_____   _____

_____   _____

_____   _____

A	B	C
intelligent	complained about	too demanding.
clever	grumbled about	humorless.
dumb	didn't enjoy	dull.
smart	griped about	mean.

E. Ask Your Partner

Ask your partner the following questions. Write the answers in the space provided.

	Yes	No
1. Are you married?	_____	_____
2. Do you have a lot of friends?	_____	_____
3. Do you think it is easy to make friends with the opposite sex?	_____	_____
4. In your country are most marriages arranged by the family?	_____	_____
5. Have you ever written a love letter?	_____	_____
6. Have you ever fallen in love at first sight?	_____	_____
7. Do you know many happily married couples?	_____	_____
8. At what age do women in your country usually get married?	_____	
9. How old was your mother when she got married?	_____	
10. What is the most romantic city in the world?	_____	

F. Put It in Writing

Write ten complete sentences about your partner, using the information you have learned in Exercise E.

> **Example:** If your partner answered **NO** to the first question you will write: He isn't married.

Have You Heard This One?

WHAT DID ONE TOOTH SAY TO THE OTHER TOOTH?

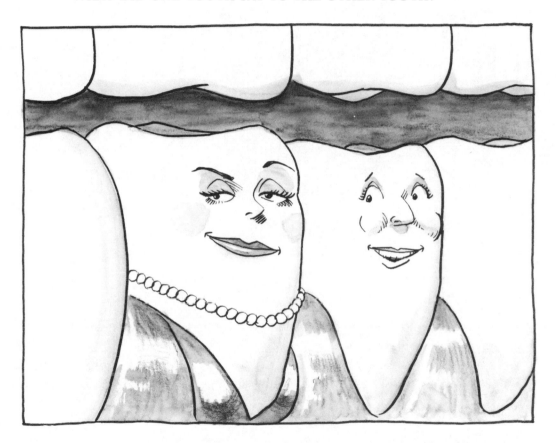

I understand that the dentist is going to take you out tonight!

5 The Vacation in Florida

One cold day in the middle of winter, Mr. and Mrs. Ross decided to fly to Florida for a vacation.

Mrs. Ross packed their summer clothes very carefully the night before their departure, and the next morning they got up early and drove directly to the airport.

While they were waiting at the check-in counter, Mr. Ross began to question his wife about the things she had packed.

"Did you remember my red bathing suit?" he asked.

"Of course," she answered.

"You didn't forget our tennis shoes, did you?" he asked.

"Of course not," she replied. Suddenly there was a long silence.

"Murray, what's wrong?" said Mrs. Ross. "You look worried."

"I'll bet you didn't bring the piano," he replied.

"The piano?" she said. "Why on earth would I bring the piano?"

"Because," he said sheepishly, "I left our plane tickets on top of it."

A. Listen and Complete

Listen to your teacher read the story and fill in the missing words in the spaces indicated.

_____ day _____ middle

_____ winter, Mr. and Mrs. Ross decided

_____ fly _____ Florida

_____ vacation.

Mrs. Ross packed _____ summer clothes very

_____ the night _____ their departure,

_____ next morning they got _____ early

_____ drove _____ airport.

While they _____ waiting _____

check-in counter, Mr. Ross began to question _____ wife

_____ things she _____ packed.

"_____ remember _____ red bathing

suit?" _____ .

"_____ course," _____ answered.

"_____ didn't forget _____ tennis

shoes, _____ you?" _____ asked.

"Of course _____," she _____. Sud-

denly there _____ long _____ .

"Murray, _____ wrong?" said Mrs. Ross.

"_____ look _____."

"_____ bet _____ didn't bring

_____ piano," _____ replied.

"The piano?" _____. "Why _____

would _____ bring _____ piano?"

"Because," _____ sheepishly, "I left

_____ plane tickets _____."

B. What Do You Think?

Circle the best answer to each of the following questions.

1. How were Mr. and Mrs. Ross planning to travel?
   - a) by car
   - b) by plane
   - c) they were planning to hitchhike

2. Why were they going to Florida?
   - a) to retire
   - b) on business
   - c) on vacation

3. Why was Mr. Ross nervous?
   - a) he was afraid to fly
   - b) he had forgotten their tickets
   - c) he had forgotten to turn off the stove

C. Words

Study the words below. Indicate in the spaces provided whether they are similar (S) or opposite (O) to the words in the boxes.

CAREFUL	
casual	_____
careless	_____
sloppy	_____
cautious	_____

WORRIED	
nervous	_____
calm	_____
uneasy	_____
relaxed	_____

SHEEPISH	
embarrassed	_____
ashamed	_____
confident	_____
secure	_____

D. Mix and Match

Complete the following sentences in four different ways. Use any vocabulary you like from lists A, B, and C.

A   B

One summer _____ decided to _____ to Florida,

_____   _____

_____   _____

_____   _____

C

but he had to return home because he had forgotten his _____

_____

_____

_____

A	B	C
a young man	fly	medicine.
a tired old man	drive	water skis.
a businessman	hitchhike	briefcase.
a photographer	sail	camera.

E.   Ask Your Partner

Ask your partner the following questions. Write the answers in the space provided.

	Yes	No
1. Do you like to travel?	____	____
2. Did you take a vacation last year?	____	____
3. Are you afraid of airplanes?	____	____
4. Have you ever been airsick?	____	____
5. Have you ever visited Florida?	____	____
6. Do you like to travel alone?	____	
7. Where would you like to go for a nice summer vacation?	____	
8. How long would you like to stay?	____	
9. Who would you like to go with?	____	
10. What is the most important thing you would take with you?	____	

F.   Put It in Writing

Write ten complete sentences about your partner, using the information you have learned in Exercise E.

> **Example:** If your partner answered **YES** to the first question, you will write: He likes to travel.

Have You Heard This One?

**WHY DID THE WOMAN WITH INSOMNIA TIPTOE PAST
THE MEDICINE CHEST?**

She didn't want to wake up the sleeping pills!

6 The Ball-Point Pen

One day a young mother was playing with her five-year-old son. Suddenly he grabbed her ball-point pen and swallowed it.

"Oh no!" cried the woman. "We must find a doctor."

She took her son, ran out of the house, put him in their car, and drove quickly to the nearest doctor's office. Taking her son by the hand, she rushed into the waiting room and shouted to the nurse, "I must see the doctor immediately."

"I'm sorry," said the nurse calmly, "but the doctor is busy."

"But nurse," she said, "please! My son just swallowed my ball-point pen!"

"Well," said the nurse, "I'm terribly sorry, but you'll just have to use a pencil."

A. Listen and Complete

Listen to your teacher read the story and fill in the missing words in the spaces indicated.

_____ day _____ mother
_____ playing with _____ five-year-old
son. _____ he grabbed _____ ball-point
pen _____ swallowed_____ .
    "Oh no!" _____ woman. "We _____
find _____ doctor."
    She took _____ son, ran _____ house,
put _____ car, _____ drove quickly
_____ nearest doctor's office. Taking
_____ son _____ hand,
_____ rushed _____ waiting room
_____ shouted _____ nurse, "I
_____ see _____ doctor immediately."
    "I'm sorry," _____ nurse calmly, "but the
_____ busy."
    "But nurse," _____ , "please! _____
son _____ swallowed _____ ball-point
pen!"
    "Well," _____ nurse, "I'm terribly sorry,
_____ you'll _____
_____ use _____ pencil."

B. What Do You Think?

Circle the best answer to each of the following questions.

1. What did the little boy swallow?
   - a) a safety pin
   - b) a penny
   - c) his mother's pen

2. Why was the boy's mother so upset?
   - a) it was her favorite pen
   - b) she was worried about her son
   - c) she didn't have a pencil

3. Why was the nurse so calm?
   - a) children swallowed pens every day
   - b) she didn't think it was dangerous
   - c) she didn't understand the problem

C. Learning New Words

Study the words below. Indicate in the spaces provided whether they are similar (S) or opposite (O) to the words in the boxes.

TO GRAB		
to take quickly	_____
to throw away	_____
to toss out	_____
to take hold of	_____

TO RUSH		
to take your time	_____
to hurry	_____
to slow down	_____
to speed up	_____

CALM		
peaceful	_____
excited	_____
quiet	_____
hysterical	_____

D. Mix and Match

Complete the following sentence in four different ways. Use any vocabulary you like from lists A, B, and C.

A middle-aged lady was playing with her grandchild one morning when suddenly he

A	B	C

_____ a big _____ and _____ it.

_____ _____ _____

_____ _____ _____

_____ _____ _____

A	B	C
grabbed	lamp	drank
snatched	bar of soap	kicked
took hold of	dog	ate
picked up	bottle of beer	broke

E. Ask Your Partner

Ask your partner the following questions. Write the answers in the space provided.

	Yes	No
1. Have you ever taken care of a small child?	_____	_____
2. Do you like babies?	_____	_____
3. Are there any small children in your family?	_____	_____
4. Do you think that boys are more difficult to raise than girls?	_____	_____
5. Would you like to have a large family?	_____	_____
6. Are you an only child?	_____	_____
7. Are you generally a calm person?	_____	_____
8. Do you usually panic in an emergency?	_____	_____
9. Did you ever swallow anything dangerous when you were a child?	_____	_____
10. Would you rather be a child than an adult?	_____	_____

F. Put It in Writing

Write ten complete sentences about your partner, using the information you have learned in Exercise E.

Example: If your partner answered **YES** to the first question, you will write: He has taken care of a small child.

Have You Heard This One?

WHAT DID THE BIG BALL-POINT PEN SAY
TO THE LITTLE PENCIL?

You're pretty sharp for such a little fellow!

7 Men and Lions

A man and a lion were having an argument one day.

"A man is stronger than a lion," said the man.

"No, No. A lion is stronger than a man," said the lion.

"A man is more intelligent than a lion," said the man.

"Don't be stupid. A lion is more intelligent than a man," said the lion.

"Lions are not as beautiful as men," said the man.

"You must be joking," said the lion. "Lions are much more beautiful than men."

"But look," said the man, "I'll prove it to you." And he took the lion to a museum and showed him all the paintings and statues of handsome, powerful men conquering lions.

The lion looked at all the great works of art for a long time, then turned to the man and asked, "Who did these paintings?"

"A man, of course," said the man.

"And who made all these statues?" asked the lion.

"Men made them. Great men! Powerful men!" said the man.

"Just as I thought," said the lion, "but showing me these works of art doesn't help your argument at all."

"What do you mean?" said the man.

"Don't you see?" said the lion. "These have all been made from a man's point of view. Imagine how different they would be if the artists had been lions."

A.   Listen and Complete

Listen to your teacher read the story and fill in the missing words in the spaces indicated.

_____ man _____ lion _____ having _____ argument _____ day.

"_____ man is _____ lion," said _____ man.

"No, No. _____ lion _____ stronger _____ man," said _____ lion.

"_____ man _____ intelligent _____ lion," said _____ man.

"Don't _____ stupid. _____ lion _____ intelligent _____ man," said _____ lion.

"Lions _____ beautiful _____ men," said _____ man.

"You _____ joking," said _____ lion. "Lions _____ beautiful _____ men."

"_____ look," _____ man, "I'll prove _____ ." And _____ took _____ lion _____ museum _____ showed _____ paintings _____ statues _____ handsome, powerful men conquering lions.

_____ lion looked _____ great works _____ art _____ long time _____ turned _____ man _____ , "Who did _____ paintings?"

"_____ man, _____ ," said _____ man.

"And _____ made _____ statues?" _____ lion.

"Men made _____ . _____ men! Powerful men!" _____ man.

"_____ thought," said _____ lion, " _____ showing _____ works _____ art doesn't help _____ argument _____ ."

"What _____ mean?" _____ man.

"Don't _____ ?" said _____ lion. " _____ have _____ made _____ man's point _____ view. Imagine _____ different _____ would _____ artists _____ lions."

B.   What Do You Think?

Circle the best answer to each of the following questions.

1.   What were the man and the lion arguing about?
   a) which came first, the chicken or the egg
   b) the superiority of men to animals
   c) women's rights

2.   What did the lion say to the man?
   a) that lions were more fun than men
   b) that lions were more intelligent than men
   c) nothing

3.   Where did the man take the lion?
   a) he took him home
   b) he took him to the movies
   c) he took him to a museum

C.   Learning New Words

Study the words below. Indicate in the spaces provided whether they are similar (S) or opposite (O) to the words in the boxes.

TO ARGUE		
	to fight with words	_____
	to disagree	_____
	to take the opposite point of view	_____
	to have the same idea	_____

TO CONQUER		
	to overcome	_____
	to beat	_____
	to surrender	_____
	to give up	_____

HANDSOME		
	good-looking	_____
	homely	_____
	attractive	_____
	ugly	_____

D.   Mix and Match

Complete the following sentences in four different ways. Use any vocabulary you like from lists A, B, and C.

A

Jack's cousin gave him a _____ for his birthday.

_____

_____

_____

B   C

He _____ because he _____

_____   _____

_____   _____

_____   _____

A	B	C
cat	took it to the zoo	didn't have room for it.
stuffed bear	kept it	hated it.
monkey	sold it	loved it.
bird	gave it to a friend	was allergic to it.

E. Ask Your Partner

Ask your partner the following questions. Write the answers in the space provided.

	Yes	No
1. Is a wild animal more dangerous than a crazy man?	_____	_____
2. Have you ever seen a lion?	_____	_____
3. Are there many statues of lions in your country?	_____	_____
4. Would you like to have a baby lion for a house pet?	_____	_____
5. Have you ever gone on a safari?	_____	_____
6. Do you believe in the saying, "A cat has nine lives"?	_____	_____
7. Do you enjoy going to the zoo?	_____	_____
8. In your opinion, what is the most beautiful animal in the world?	_____	
9. Which animal is a symbol of strength in your country?	_____	
10. If you could be an animal, which one would you like to be?	_____	

F. Put It in Writing

Write ten complete sentences about your partner, using the information you have learned in Exercise E.

Example: If your partner answered **YES** to the first question you will write:
He thinks that a wild animal is more dangerous than a crazy man.

Have You Heard This One?

**WHAT DID THE WALL-TO-WALL CARPET SAY
TO THE FLOOR?**

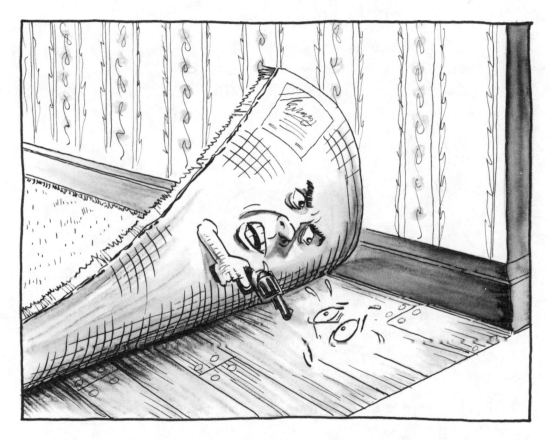

Don't move! I've got you covered.

8 Dreams

Three students were talking one day about their dreams for the future.

One of the students was a struggling young painter. The second was planning a career in the business world, and the third was studying philosophy.

"I'd like to be as famous as Picasso," said the painter.

"I'd like to be as rich and powerful as Rockefeller," said the business student.

The student of philosophy waited for a few moments before he spoke, and then he looked at the other two and said very quietly, "You know there are only two great tragedies in life."

"What do you mean?" said the others.

"Well," he said, "the first is *not* to get the thing you want the most in life."

"And what is the second?" they asked.

"The second," he replied, "is to get it."

A. Listen and Complete

Listen to your teacher read the story and fill in the missing words in the spaces indicated.

_____ students _____ talking one day
about _____ dreams _____ future.
_____ students _____ struggling
_____ painter. The second _____
planning _____ career _____ business
world, _____ third _____ studying
philosophy.

"_____ like to be _____ famous
_____ Picasso," said _____ painter.

"_____ be _____ rich
_____ powerful _____ Rockefeller,"
_____ business student.

_____ student _____ philosophy
waited _____ moments _____ spoke,
_____ he looked _____ two
_____ said very _____, "You know
_____ only two great _____ life."

"What _____ mean?" said _____
others.

"Well," _____ said, "the _____ is
_____ get _____ you want
_____ most _____ life."

"And _____ second?" _____ asked.

"_____," _____ replied, "is
_____."

B. What Do You Think?

Circle the best answer to each of the following questions.

1. What were the three students discussing?
    - a) their dreams for the future
    - b) how to win at poker
    - c) how to meet girls

2. What was the young painter's dream?
    - a) to live in Paris
    - b) to be as famous as Picasso
    - c) to marry a rich woman

3. What was the business student's dream?
    - a) to open his own pizza parlor
    - b) to rob a bank
    - c) to be as rich as Rockefeller

C. Learning New Words

Complete each sentence in four different ways. Indicate in the spaces provided whether each answer is True (T) or False (F).

1. If a person is **STRUGGLING** to learn English, he is
    trying very hard _____
    not trying at all _____
    making a serious effort _____
    probably doing his best _____

2. If a person is **POWERFUL**, he or she is probably
    not afraid of anything _____
    scared of the dark _____
    influential _____
    timid _____

3. If a person is **FAMOUS**, he or she is probably
    easily recognized _____
    difficult to meet _____
    boring _____
    stupid _____

D. Mix and Match

Complete the following sentence in four different ways. Use any vocabulary you like from lists A, B, and C.

A

All his life, he wanted to _____

_____

_____

_____

B   C

but _____ because _____

_____   _____

_____   _____

_____   _____

A	B	C
climb Mt. Everest, become a movie star, sail around the world, make a million dollars,	he never did it he couldn't do it it was impossible it was out of the question	it was too difficult. his health was poor. it was too expensive. he didn't have any talent.

E. Ask Your Partner

Ask your partner the following questions. Write the answers in the space provided.

		Yes	No
1.	Do you often dream about the future?	_____	_____
2.	Do you believe that dreams can come true?	_____	_____
3.	Do you think it is difficult to be successful in life?	_____	_____
4.	Have you ever studied philosophy?	_____	_____
5.	Are you an optimistic person?	_____	_____
6.	Are you happier now that you were five years ago?	_____	_____
7.	Do you think your life would be easier if you were famous?	_____	_____
8.	Do you often think about your past?	_____	_____
9.	Would you like to re-live your childhood?	_____	_____
10.	What famous person do you admire?	_____	

F. Put It in Writing

Write ten complete sentences about your partner, using the information you have learned in Exercise E.

Example: If your partner answered **YES** to the first question, you will write:
He likes to dream about his future.

Have You Heard This One?

WHAT DID THE SALT AND PEPPER SAY TO EACH OTHER
AS THEY WERE LOOKING AT THE HAMBURGER PATTY?

Let's shake on it!

9 Income Tax

One day a teacher was giving her young students a lesson on how the government works. She was trying to explain the principle of income tax.

"You see," she began, speaking slowly and carefully, "each person who works must pay part of his or her salary to the government. If you make a high salary, your taxes are high. If you don't make much money, your taxes are low."

"Is that clear?" she asked. "Does everyone understand the meaning of income tax?" The students nodded.

"Are there any questions?" she asked. The students shook their heads.

"Very good," she said. "Now, I would like you to take a piece of paper and write a short paragraph on the subject of income tax."

Little Joey was a slow learner. He had lots of problems with spelling and grammar, but this time at least he seemed to understand the assignment. He grabbed his pen and after a few minutes, he handed the teacher the following composition:

Once I had a dog. His name was Tax.
I opened the door and in come Tax.

A.   Listen and Complete

Listen to your teacher read the story and fill in the missing words in the spaces indicated.

_____ day _____ teacher _____ giving _____ young students _____ lesson _____ how _____ government works. She _____ trying _____ explain _____ principle _____ income tax.

   "You see," _____ began, speaking _____ carefully, "_____ person _____ works _____ pay _____ salary _____ government. If _____ make _____ high salary, _____ taxes _____ high. If _____ make _____ money, _____ taxes _____ low."

   "_____ clear?" she asked. "_____ everyone understand _____ meaning _____ income tax?" _____ students _____ .

   "_____ any questions?" _____ asked. _____ students shook _____ heads.

   "Very good," _____ . "Now, I _____ you _____ piece _____ paper _____ write _____ short paragraph _____ subject of income tax."

   Little Joey _____ slow learner. He had _____ problems _____ spelling _____ grammar, _____ time _____ he _____ understand _____ assignment. _____ grabbed _____ pen _____ after _____ minutes, _____ handed _____ teacher _____ following composition:

Once I had a dog. His name was Tax.
I opened the door and in come Tax.

B. What Do You Think?

Circle the best answer to each of the following questions.

1. What was the teacher trying to explain?
    - a) the basic principles of the tax system
    - b) the past tense of irregular verbs
    - c) how to raise chickens at home

2. What did the teacher ask the students to do?
    - a) take a fifteen-minute nap
    - b) tear up their papers and go home
    - c) write a paragraph on "income tax"

3. What did little Joey do?
    - a) carved his name on the top of the desk
    - b) made a paper airplane
    - c) wrote a paragraph on "income tax"

C. Learning New Words

Study the words below. Indicate in the spaces provided whether they are similar (S) or opposite (O) to the words in the boxes.

TO HAND	
to give	_____
to receive	_____
to pass	_____
to keep	_____

TO NOD	
to shake your head	_____
to agree	_____
to say "yes"	_____
to disagree	_____

TO EXPLAIN	
to describe	_____
to question	_____
to ask about	_____
to tell about	_____

D. Mix and Match

Complete the following sentence in four different ways. Use any vocabulary you like from lists A, B, and C.

A   B

The _____ student _____

    _____   _____

    _____   _____

    _____   _____

C

the teacher and _____ the assignment immediately.

    _____

    _____

    _____

A	B	C
bright	listened to	did
excellent	paid attention to	finished
poor	didn't listen to	forgot
foolish	laughed at	didn't do

E. Ask Your Partner

Ask your partner the following questions. Write the answers in the space provided.

	Yes	No
1. Would you like to be a teacher?	_____	_____
2. Is anyone in your family a teacher?	_____	_____
3. Are teachers well paid in your country?	_____	_____
4. Are you good in math?	_____	_____
5. Did you ever fail a subject in school?	_____	_____
6. Have you ever studied algebra?	_____	_____
7. What was your favorite subject in high school?	_____	
8. Was your first teacher a woman or a man?	_____	
9. What was your most difficult subject in high school?	_____	
10. How old were you when you started first grade?	_____	

F. Put It in Writing

Write ten complete sentences about your partner, using the information you have learned in Exercise E.

Example: If your partner answered **YES** to the first question you will write: He would like to be a teacher.

Have You Heard This One?

WHAT HAS FOUR WHEELS AND FLIES?

A garbage truck!

10 Daddy's Little Girl

One evening a little girl was sitting with her father in the living room. They were both reading. He was reading the newspaper and she was reading a book, but every once in a while she found a word that she didn't understand and asked him to explain it to her.

"Daddy," she said, "what's a gossip?"

"A gossip," said her father, "is someone who repeats unpleasant things about other people, someone who talks about people behind their back."

"Oh," she said, "you mean like Mrs. Stein."

"That's right," said her father, and he continued reading his paper.

A few moments later, she interrupted him again.

"Daddy," she said, "what's a bore?"

"A bore," said her father, trying to be patient, "is a person who is *not* interesting, a person who talks about himself all the time, for example."

"Oh, you mean someone like Mr. Kelly?" she asked.

"Exactly," answered her father, returning to his paper.

"Daddy?" she said, with a question in her voice.

"Yes?" said her father, losing his patience. "What is it now?"

"Daddy," said the little girl, "what's a pain in the neck?"

Her father put down his newspaper, looked at her tenderly, and said, "A pain in the neck is a little girl who keeps asking her father questions while he's trying to read the newspaper."

A. Listen and Complete

Listen to your teacher read the story and fill in the missing words in the spaces indicated.

_____ evening _____ girl _____ sitting _____ father _____ living room. _____ reading. He _____ reading _____ newspaper _____ she _____ reading _____ book, _____ once _____ she found _____ that _____ understand _____ asked _____ explain _____ to _____.

    "Daddy," _____, "_____ gossip?"

    "_____ gossip," _____ father, "_____ someone _____ repeats unpleasant things _____ people, someone _____ talks _____ people _____ back."

    "Oh," _____, "You _____ Mrs. Stein."

    "That's _____," said _____ father, _____ continued reading _____ paper.

    A _____ moments _____, _____ interrupted _____.

    "Daddy," _____, "What's _____ bore?"

    "A bore," said _____ father, trying _____ patient, "_____ person _____ *not* interesting, _____ person _____ about himself _____ time, _____ example."

    "Oh, _____ someone _____ Mr. Kelly?" _____.

    "_____," answered _____ father, returning _____ paper.

    "Daddy?" _____, with _____ question _____ voice.

    "Yes?" _____ father, losing _____ patience. "What _____ now?"

    "Daddy," _____ little girl, "what's _____ pain _____ neck?"

    _____ father put down _____ newspaper, looked _____ tenderly, _____, "A pain _____ neck _____ girl _____ keeps asking _____ father questions _____ trying _____ read _____ newspaper."

B. What Do You Think?

Circle the best answer to each of the following questions.

1. What was the little girl's father doing?
    a) he was taking a nap
    b) he was reading a newspaper
    c) he was watching TV

2. What was the little girl doing?
    a) she was listening carefully to her father
    b) she was answering her father's questions
    c) she was asking her father questions

3. What did the little girl's father do when she asked him so many questions?
    a) he ignored her
    b) he tried to answer her
    c) he threw his newspaper on the floor and left

C. Learning New Words

Complete each sentence in four different ways. Indicate in the spaces provided whether each answer is True (T) or False (F).

1. You are probably a **BORE** if
    you always talk about yourself   _____
    you tell the same stories over and over   _____
    your friends fall asleep while you are talking   _____
    everybody listens carefully when you speak   _____

2. You are a very **PATIENT** person if
    you don't mind waiting in line   _____
    you call your friends back if the line is busy   _____
    you get angry when someone is late   _____
    you love to plant seeds in a garden   _____

3. If people are **GOSSIPING** about you, they are probably
    saying something unpleasant   _____
    saying something nice   _____
    criticizing you   _____
    enjoying themselves   _____

D. Mix and Match

Complete the following sentence in four different ways. Use any vocabulary you like from lists A, B, and C.

A

The tired businessman was trying to _____ but it was

_____

_____

_____

almost impossible because his

B   C

_____ kept _____

_____   _____

_____   _____

_____   _____

A	B	C
think	little daughter	interrupting him.
take a nap	wife	talking to him.
finish a report	secretary	annoying him.
make a long-distance call	dog	asking him questions.

E. Ask Your Partner

Ask your partner the following questions. Write the answers in the space provided.

	Yes	No
1. Are you often impatient?	____	____
2. Do your friends sometimes annoy you?	____	____
3. Do you often interrupt a conversation when another person is speaking?	____	____
4. Are you a good listener?	____	____
5. Do you often ask questions in class?	____	____
6. Did you ask a lot of questions when you were a child?	____	____
7. Do you like to gossip?	____	____
8. Do you agree that "children should be seen but not heard"?	____	____
9. Is your teacher a patient person?	____	____
10. Who usually answered your questions when you were a child?	_____	

F. Put It in Writing

Write ten complete sentences about your partner, using the information you have learned in Exercise E.

Example: If your partner answered **YES** to the first question, you will write: He is often impatient.

Have You Heard This One?

WHAT DID THE BIG MAMA SCISSORS SAY
TO THE LITTLE BABY SCISSORS?

Aw, cut it out!

11 *Margie and Paul*

Margie and Paul were very close friends, but there were times when they didn't get along at all.

Paul was a wonderful man, but there were certain things about him that drove Margie crazy. He had a marvelous sense of humor, but he was extremely conceited and often drank too much.

Margie was not an easy person to get along with either. She was very critical, self-centered, and hard to please.

One night after dinner, Margie was so tired of Paul she turned to him and said, "You know, Paul, frankly, if you were my husband I would poison your coffee."

"Well, to tell you the truth, Margie," he replied, "if you were my wife, I'd drink it."

A. Listen and Complete

Listen to your teacher read the story and fill in the missing words in the spaces indicated.

_____ Margie _____ Paul

_____ close friends, _____ were times

_____ didn't _____ along

_____ all.

Paul _____ wonderful man, _____

certain _____ about _____ drove Margie

_____ . He _____ marvelous

_____ humor, _____ extremely conceited

_____ often drank _____ much.

Margie _____ easy person _____

along _____ either. She _____ critical,

_____ , and hard to please.

_____ night _____ dinner, Margie

_____ tired _____ Paul

_____ turned _____ and said,

"_____ know, Paul, _____ , if

_____ husband I _____ poison

_____ coffee."

"Well, _____ tell _____ truth, Mar-

gie," _____ replied, "if _____ my wife,

_____ drink _____ ."

B. What Do You Think?

Circle the best answer to each of the following questions.

1. Why did Margie criticize Paul?
   - a) he never laughed at her jokes
   - b) he bored her
   - c) he drank too much

2. Why did Paul criticize Margie?
   - a) her coffee tasted like dishwater
   - b) she never listened to him
   - c) she was self-centered

3. What did Margie say she would do if she were married to Paul?
   - a) commit suicide
   - b) murder him
   - c) go home to mother

C. Learning New Words

Study the words below. Indicate in the spaces provided whether they are similar (S) or opposite (O) to the words in the boxes.

TO GET ALONG WITH	
to enjoy the company of	_____
to be on good terms with	_____
to have a pleasant relationship with	_____
to have problems with	_____

TO DRIVE CRAZY	
to annoy	_____
to bother a lot	_____
to get on someone's nerves	_____
to enjoy something	_____

MARVELOUS	
wonderful	_____
terrific	_____
terrible	_____
splendid	_____

D. Mix and Match

Complete the following sentence in four different ways. Use any vocabulary you like from lists A, B, and C.

A	B

One day _____ man met _____ woman,

_____   _____

_____   _____

_____   _____

but when he asked her to marry him, she refused because he was

C

_____

_____

_____

_____

A	B	C
a handsome	a 90-year-old	too old.
an 80-year-old	a gorgeous	too young.
a 20-year-old	a brilliant	too short.
a smart	a tall	too dumb.

E. Ask Your Partner

Ask your partner the following questions. Write the answers in the space provided.

	Yes	No
1. Are you very critical of other people?	_____	_____
2. Are you very critical of yourself?	_____	_____
3. Do you have any bad habits?	_____	_____
4. Did your mother criticize you a lot when you were a child?	_____	_____
5. Does your father have a good sense of humor?	_____	_____
6. Do you drink?	_____	_____
7. Do you enjoy most of the people you meet?	_____	_____
8. How long does it take to get to know a person really well?	_____	
9. How long do you think two people should know each other before they get married?	_____	
10. How long have you known your best friend?	_____	

F. Put It in Writing

Write ten complete sentences about your partner, using the information you have learned in Exercise E.

Example: If your partner answered **YES** to the first question, you will write:
He is very critical of other people.

Have You Heard This One?

**WHAT DID THE LITTLE CHIMNEY SAY
TO THE BIG CHIMNEY?**

You smoke too much!

12 The Dog at the Movies

A woman was sitting by herself in a movie theater. The movie she was about to see was a musical version of a very successful book that had sold a million copies that year.

As the woman was waiting for the movie to begin, she noticed that the theater was very crowded but the two seats next to her were empty.

Suddenly, a large man carrying a big fur coat walked down the aisle and sat down, placing the fur on the seat next to her.

When the lights went out, the fur coat began to move, and the woman realized it was not a coat but a large furry dog. He was sitting up in the seat, watching the movie screen with great interest. As soon as the movie started, the dog began to nod his head and beat his paws in perfect time to the music.

When the movie was over the woman turned to the man and said, "Excuse me, sir, but I've never seen such a well-behaved dog in a movie theater before. Does he go to the movies often?"

"Oh, yes," replied the man.

"And he seemed to enjoy everything so much," she said. "It was just amazing!"

"Frankly, it surprised me, too," said the man. "He hated the book."

A. Listen and Complete

Listen to your teacher read the story and fill in the missing words in the spaces indicated.

_____ woman _____ sitting _____ herself _____
movie theater. The movie _____ about _____ see _____
musical version _____ very successful book _____ sold
_____ million copies _____ year.

_____ woman _____ waiting _____ movie
_____ begin, _____ noticed _____ theater
_____ crowded _____ seats next _____ were empty.
Suddenly, _____ man carrying _____ fur coat walked
_____ aisle _____ down, placing _____ on the seat
_____ her.

_____ the lights _____ , _____ fur coat
_____ to move, _____ woman realized _____ coat
_____ large furry dog. _____ sitting _____ seat, watching
_____ movie screen _____ great interest. _____ movie
started, _____ dog began _____ his head _____ beat
_____ paws _____ perfect time _____ music.

_____ movie _____ over _____ woman turned
_____ man and said, "Excuse me, sir, _____ I've never seen
_____ well-behaved dog _____ movie theater before. Does
_____ go _____ movies often?"

"Oh yes," _____ the man.

"And _____ to enjoy everything _____ much," _____
said. "It _____ just amazing."

"Frankly, _____ me _____ ," said the man. " _____
hated _____ book."

B. What Do You Think?

Circle the best answer to each of the following questions.

1. Why was the woman surprised?
    a) she saw a large dog sitting next to her
    b) she saw a large man sitting next to her
    c) somebody stole her fur coat

2. What was the dog doing at the movies?
    a) sleeping
    b) eating popcorn
    c) watching the movie

3. What did the woman do when the movie was over?
    a) she picked up the dog and left
    b) she stayed and spoke with the man
    c) she called the manager to complain about the dog

C. Learning New Words

Study the words below. Indicate in the spaces provided whether they are similar (S) or opposite (O) to the words in the boxes.

FRANK		
honest	_____
truthful	_____
sincere	_____
dishonest	_____

TO REALIZE		
to comprehend correctly	_____
to understand	_____
to dawn on	_____
to misunderstand	_____

PERFECT		
wrong	_____
exactly right	_____
correct	_____
flawless	_____

D. Mix and Match

Complete the following sentence in four different ways. Use any vocabulary you like from lists A, B, and C.

A

One day _____ went to the movies, sat down,

_____

_____

_____

B   C

and suddenly _____ that _____

_____   _____

_____   _____

_____   _____

A	B	C
a woman	saw	the theater was empty.
a young child	realized	the movie was over.
a man	noticed	her father was sitting in the next seat.
a dog	understood	a dog was sitting in the next seat.

E. Ask Your Partner

Ask your partner the following questions. Write the answers in the space provided.

	Yes	No
1. Do you like movies?	_____	_____
2. Have you ever cried at a movie?	_____	_____
3. Would you like to be a movie star?	_____	_____
4. Are you planning to go to the movies tomorrow night?	_____	_____
5. Have you ever fallen asleep in a movie?	_____	_____
6. How much does a movie ticket cost in your country?	_____	
7. Who's your favorite movie star?	_____	
8. How often do you go to the movies?	_____	
9. What kind of a story do you like the best: a comedy, a love story, or a mystery?	_____	
10. What was the name of the first movie you ever saw?	_____	

F. Put It in Writing

Write ten complete sentences about your partner, using the information you have learned in Exercise E.

> **Example:** If your partner answered **YES** to the first question you will write:
> He likes movies.

Have You Heard This One?

**WHAT DID THE BOY CANDLE SAY TO
THE GIRL CANDLE?**

I'd love to go out with you!

13 A Visit with Grandma Moses

One day a woman went to visit the studio of Grandma Moses, the famous American artist. The charming old painter was then in her late eighties, but she was still very active and full of life. She seemed to enjoy showing her paintings to her visitor, who was thrilled to be in the presence of so much beauty.

"Oh my!" cried the visitor. "Those colors! Those gorgeous colors! How I wish I could take them home with me."

"You will, you will," said Grandma Moses with a sweet smile.

"What do you mean?" asked the visitor.

"Well," said Grandma, "you're sitting on my brushes."

A. Listen and Complete

Listen to your teacher read the story and fill in the missing words in the spaces indicated.

_____ day _____ woman went
_____ the studio _____ Grandma Moses,
_____ American artist. _____ charming
_____ painter _____ in her
_____ eighties, _____ was still
_____ active _____ full
_____ . She _____ to enjoy showing
_____ paintings _____ visitor,
_____ thrilled _____ presence
_____ beauty.

"Oh my!" cried _____ visitor. "_____
colors! Those gorgeous _____! How I
_____ I _____ take
_____ home _____ me."

"You _____, you will,"
Grandma Moses _____ sweet smile.

"What _____ mean?" asked _____
visitor.

"Well," _____ Grandma, "you're sitting
_____ brushes."

B. What Do You Think?

Circle the best answer to each of the following questions.

1. What was Grandma Moses like?
   - a) she was cold and unfriendly
   - b) she was charming and full of life
   - c) she was conceited

2. What were her paintings like?
   - a) they were gorgeous
   - b) they were difficult to understand
   - c) they were ugly

3. What was the visitor doing?
   - a) she was admiring the paintings
   - b) she was admiring the furniture
   - c) she was arguing over the price of a painting

C. Learning New Words

Complete each sentence in four different ways. Indicate in the spaces provided whether each answer is True (T) or False (F).

1. Someone who is **FULL OF LIFE** usually has

lots of friends	_____
lots of time	_____
no interests	_____
many interests	_____

2. A person might be **THRILLED** if he or she

won first prize in a contest	_____
found $1000 on the street	_____
got fired	_____
got a wonderful job	_____

3. If you have a **GORGEOUS** smile, you are probably

a friendly person	_____
an unfriendly person	_____
lots of fun	_____
brilliant	_____

D. Mix and Match

Complete the following sentences in four different ways. Use any vocabulary you like from lists A, B, and C.

A

My grandmother is a _____ person.

_____

_____

_____

B   C

She is _____ but she still _____

_____   _____

_____   _____

_____   _____

A	B	C
remarkable	in her late eighties	leads a very
extraordinary	in her nineties	active life.
unusual	a hundred and	plays tennis every
fabulous	one	day.
	in her seventies	loves to garden.
		enjoys life.

E. Ask Your Partner

Ask your partner the following questions. Write the answers in the space provided.

	Yes	No
1. Are your grandparents alive?	_____	_____
2. Do you have any relatives who are over eighty years old?	_____	_____
3. Would you like to live to be ninety?	_____	_____
4. Are you afraid of growing old?	_____	_____
5. Do you believe that "life begins at forty"?	_____	_____
6. Do you think that elderly parents should live with their children?	_____	_____
7. Do women in your country usually live longer than men?	_____	_____
8. What do you think is the best age in life?	_____	
9. How long does an average man in your country usually live?	_____	
10. What is the best age for a person to retire?	_____	

F. Put It in Writing

Write ten complete sentences about your partner, using the information you have learned in Exercise E.

> **Example:** If your partner answered **YES** to the first question, you will write: His grandparents are alive.

Have You Heard This One?

WHAT DID THE OLD LEATHER SUITCASE SAY TO
THE LITTLE IRON BOX?

I'd rather wear out than rust!

14 The Entertainer

An extremely wealthy woman was planning an intimate dinner party and decided to hire a professional musician to entertain her guests. She asked her secretary to contact a famous pianist and make all the arrangements.

The secretary called a distinguished musician to discuss the details of the party.

"Now, sir," she said, "we expect you to arrive at 7:30 sharp."

"Certainly," he said.

"Of course you will wear black tie, won't you?" she asked.

"Of course," he replied.

"Now then," said the secretary, "we would like you to start with some Mozart during the fish course, then perhaps a little Chopin and a nice Beethoven sonata for dessert."

"Very well," said the artist.

"What do you charge?" she asked.

"One thousand dollars," he answered.

"That will be fine, but there is one other thing," she added.

"Yes?" he replied.

"We would appreciate it if you did *not* mingle with the guests."

"Oh," said the pianist, "in that case, I only charge five hundred."

A. Listen and Complete

Listen to your teacher read the story and fill in the missing words in the spaces indicated.

_____ wealthy woman _____ planning _____ intimate dinner party _____ decided to hire _____ professional musician _____ entertain _____ guests. _____ asked _____ secretary _____ contact _____ pianist _____ make _____ arrangements.

_____ secretary _____ distinguished musician _____ discuss _____ details _____ party.

"Now, sir," _____ said, "_____ expect _____ arrive _____ 7:30 sharp."

"Certainly," _____ .

"_____ course, you _____ black tie, _____ you?" _____ asked.

"Of course," he replied.

"Now then," _____ secretary, "_____ like you _____ start with some Mozart _____ fish course, _____ Chopin _____ Beethoven sonata _____ dessert."

"Very well," _____ artist.

"What _____ charge?" _____ asked.

"_____ thousand _____," he answered.

"_____ will _____ fine, _____ there is _____ other thing," she added.

"Yes?" _____ replied.

"_____ appreciate _____ did _____ mingle _____ guests."

"Oh," _____ pianist, "_____ case, I only charge _____ hundred."

B. What Do You Think?

Circle the best answer to each of the following questions.

1. What kind of a party was the woman planning to give?
   - a) a large cocktail party
   - b) a costume party
   - c) an intimate dinner party

2. What kind of entertainment did the woman decide to have?
   - a) 15 young men playing electric guitars
   - b) a stand-up comedian
   - c) a famous pianist

3. What did the woman ask her secretary to do?
   - a) start practicing her violin
   - b) contact a famous pianist
   - c) buy a second-hand piano

C. Learning New Words

Study the words below. Indicate in the spaces provided whether they are similar (S) or opposite (O) to the words in the boxes.

TO CONTACT	
to get in touch with	_____
to write or telephone	_____
to avoid	_____
to stay away from	_____

TO MINGLE	
to mix with	_____
to stay by yourself	_____
to hide from	_____
to join with	_____

DISTINGUISHED	
elegant	_____
plain	_____
undistinguished	_____
ordinary	_____

D. Mix and Match

Complete the following sentence in four different ways. Use any vocabulary you like from lists A, B, and C.

A   B

A very _____ was planning _____

_____   _____

_____   _____

_____   _____

C

and decided to hire _____ to entertain the guests.

_____

_____

_____

A	B	C
distinguished professor	a cocktail party	a magician
snobbish socialite	a costume party	an orchestra
elderly politician	a dinner-dance	a performing dog
wealthy doctor	a New Year's party	a string quartet

E. Ask Your Partner

Ask your partner the following questions. Write the answers in the space provided.

	Yes	No
1. Do you enjoy large parties?	_____	_____
2. Are you a good cook?	_____	_____
3. Do you like to entertain friends at home?	_____	_____
4. Have you ever given yourself a birthday party?	_____	_____
5. Have you ever gone to a surprise party?	_____	_____
6. Were you ever the guest of honor at a party?	_____	_____
7. Would you be nervous if you had to prepare a dinner party for twelve guests?	_____	_____
8. Did you celebrate your birthday last year?	_____	_____
9. Have you ever gone to a pot-luck supper?	_____	_____
10. Do you like costume parties?	_____	_____

F. Put It in Writing

Write ten complete sentences about your partner, using the information you have learned in Exercise E.

Example: If your partner answered **YES** to the first question you will write:
He enjoys large parties.

Have You Heard This One?

**WHAT DID THE LITTLE ICE CUBE SAY TO THE WOMAN
WHEN SHE OPENED THE REFRIGERATOR?**

Please close the door. It's freezing in here!

15 Keeping Up with the Joneses

When Betty and Bob first got married, they lived in a tiny little apartment in a very poor section of town. As soon as Bob got a raise, they moved to a larger apartment, and from that day on, each time Bob got a promotion they would pack up everything and move to a more expensive place.

After a while, Bob got tired of all this packing and moving, and one day he came home with a big smile on his face.

"Honey," he said, "I have wonderful news!"

"What is it?" asked Betty.

"I got another raise today!" he said.

"That's marvelous!" said Betty. "When do we move?"

"We don't have to move for a long time," said Bob.

"Why not?" said Betty. "What do you mean?"

"Well," said Bob, "the landlord just doubled our rent."

A. Listen and Complete

Listen to your teacher read the story and fill in the missing words in the spaces indicated.

_____Betty _____ Bob

_____ got married, _____ lived

_____ tiny _____ apartment

_____ poor section _____ town.

_____ soon _____ Bob

_____ raise, _____ moved

_____ apartment, _____ that day

_____, _____ time Bob

_____ promotion _____ pack up

everything _____ move _____ expensive place.

    After _____, Bob _____ tired

_____ packing _____ moving,

_____ one day _____ came home

_____ big smile _____ face.

    "Honey," _____, "I _____ wonderful
news!"

    "What _____?" asked Betty.

    "I _____ raise _____!" he said.

    "_____ marvelous!" said Betty. "When
_____ move?"

    "We _____ have _____ for
_____ time," said Bob.

    "Why _____?" said Betty. "What
_____ mean?"

    "Well," _____ Bob, "_____ landlord
_____ doubled _____ rent."

B. What Do You Think?

Circle the best answer to each of the following questions.

1. Where did Betty and Bob live when they first got married?
    a) with Betty's mother
    b) in a tiny little apartment
    c) in a mobile home

2. What did they do as soon as Bob got a raise?
    a) they got a divorce
    b) they built a house
    c) they moved to a larger apartment

3. How did Bob feel about packing and moving?
    a) he enjoyed it
    b) he was tired of it
    c) he looked forward to it

C. Learning New Words

Complete each sentence in four different ways. Indicate in the space provided whether each answer is True (T) or False (F).

1. If your boss gives you a **RAISE,** he is probably
    pleased with your work   _____
    annoyed with you   _____
    worried about you   _____
    jealous of you   _____

2. If you **GET TIRED** of doing something, you should
    take a break   _____
    try a little harder   _____
    do it a little faster   _____
    call your mother for help   _____

3. If you get a **PROMOTION,** your job will probably be
    more difficult   _____
    more complicated   _____
    easier   _____
    more important   _____

D. Mix and Match

Complete the following sentence in four different ways. Use any vocabulary you like from lists A, B, and C.

A

Mr. Jones will have to get _____ as soon as possible

_____

_____

_____

B   C

because Mrs. Jones wants _____ so that they can _____

_____   _____

_____   _____

_____   _____

A	B	C
a big raise	to drive to Florida	impress their neighbors.
a larger house	to hire a maid	enjoy life.
a better job	to buy a piano	relax on the beach.
a car	to have a large family	enjoy music at home.

E. Ask Your Partner

Ask your partner the following questions. Write the answers in the space provided.

	Yes	No
1. Are you living in a small apartment right now?	_____	_____
2. Do you enjoy packing and moving?	_____	_____
3. Are you a good packer?	_____	_____
4. Do you like old houses?	_____	_____
5. Do you find it hard to throw things away?	_____	_____
6. Do you have clothes in your closet that you never wear?	_____	_____
7. Are you a neat person?	_____	_____
8. Would you like to live in another country for a few years?	_____	_____
9. If you were going to move to another city, which city would you choose?	_____	
10. How many times have you moved in the last ten years?	_____	

F. Put It in Writing

Write ten complete sentences about your partner, using the information you have learned in Exercise E.

Example: If your partner answered **YES** to the first question you will write: He is living in a small apartment right now.

Have You Heard This One?

**WHY DID THE MORON THROW THE CLOCK
OUT THE WINDOW?**

He wanted to see time fly!

16 A Conversation with Lincoln

A young soldier was having a conversation one day with Abraham Lincoln. They were discussing the difficulties of fighting a war and the various types of weapons a man might use against the enemy.

The young man was very eager to hear President Lincoln's ideas on how to win the war.

"You know," said Lincoln, "after all these years, I have finally discovered the best way to destroy the enemy."

"What is that, Mr. President?" asked the young soldier.

"It's very simple," said Lincoln. "Make him your friend."

A. Listen and Complete

Listen to your teacher read the story and fill in the missing words in the spaces indicated.

_____ soldier _____ having
_____ conversation _____ with Abraham
Lincoln. _____ discussing _____
difficulties _____ fighting _____ war
_____ various types _____ weapons
_____ man might _____ against
_____ enemy.
_____ man _____ eager
_____ President Lincoln's _____ on
_____ win _____ war.

"You know," _____ Lincoln, "after
_____ years, I have _____ discovered
_____ best way _____ destroy
_____ enemy."

"What _____, Mr. President?" _____
young soldier.

"It's _____ simple," _____ Lincoln.
"Make _____ friend."

B. What Do You Think?

Circle the best answer to each of the following questions.

1. What was the young soldier discussing with Abraham Lincoln?
    a) his career in the army
    b) the difficulties of fighting a war
    c) the weather

2. What did Lincoln say he had discovered?
    a) a bomb in the White House
    b) the best way to start a war
    c) the best way to destroy the enemy

3. What was Lincoln's method for destroying the enemy?
    a) make him your friend
    b) shoot him
    c) capture him

C. Learning New Words

Complete each sentence in four different ways. Indicate in the spaces provided whether each answer is True (T) or False (F).

1. If you don't have any **ENEMIES** you are probably
    a very nice person   _____
    not very powerful   _____
    not very wise   _____
    very lonely   _____

2. If you are **EAGER** to join the army you probably
    like to wear a uniform   _____
    love to sleep late in the morning   _____
    enjoy good food   _____
    are young and healthy   _____

3. If you **DESTROY** your career you probably will
    have to start over   _____
    feel miserable for a while _____
    never forgive yourself _____
    laugh about it   _____

D. Mix and Match

Complete the following sentence in four different ways. Use any vocabulary you like from lists A, B, and C.

A   B

The _____ told the young man that the _____ way

_____   _____

_____   _____

_____   _____

C

to settle an argument is to _____

_____

_____

_____

A	B	C
old politician	best	fight over it.
general	worst	talk about it.
philosopher	easiest	ignore it.
lazy old man	most intelligent	compromise.

E. Ask Your Partner

Ask your partner the following questions. Write the answers in the space provided.

	Yes	No
1. Are you interested in history?	_____	_____
2. Have you ever studied world history?	_____	_____
3. Would you like to join the army?	_____	_____
4. Do women serve in the armed forces in your country?	_____	_____
5. Do you believe that world peace is possible?	_____	_____
6. Do you think that men make better soldiers than women?	_____	_____
7. Do you believe that history repeats itself?	_____	_____
8. Did you ever play with a toy gun when you were a child?	_____	_____
9. Who is the most important figure in your country's history?	_____	
10. In your opinion, what was the most tragic historical event in your country?	_____	

F. Put It in Writing

Write ten complete sentences about your partner, using the information you have learned in Exercise E.

Example: If your partner answered **YES** to the first question, you will write: He is interested in history.

Have You Heard This One?

WHAT DID THE BIG STRAWBERRY SAY TO THE LITTLE STRAWBERRY?

If you're not careful,
you're going to get yourself in a jam!

17 The Woman Who Wanted To Sing

Claire always wanted to be a singer. Music was the most important thing in her life but, to tell you the truth, she had a terrible voice. She took lessons for years, practiced every day, but in spite of all this, her voice didn't improve. Honestly, it didn't get better, it just got louder.

Her teacher finally gave up and stopped the lessons, but Claire refused to quit, and one day she decided to give a concert and invited her former teacher to attend.

The teacher was very worried about what to say after the performance. She knew it would be awful and it was. She didn't want to tell a lie, but she didn't want to hurt Claire's feelings either. Finally, she got an idea and went backstage to greet her former pupil.

"Well," said Claire, "what did you think of my performance?"

"My dear," said the teacher, "you'll never be better than you were tonight."

A. Listen and Complete

Listen to your teacher read the story and fill in the missing words in the spaces indicated.

Claire _____ wanted _____ singer. Music _____ most important thing _____ life _____, to tell you _____ truth, she _____ terrible voice. She took _____ for _____, practiced _____, but in spite of _____, her voice _____ improve. Honestly, _____ didn't get _____, it _____ got louder.

_____ teacher _____ gave up _____ stopped _____ lessons, _____ Claire refused _____, and _____ day she _____ to give _____ concert _____ her former teacher _____ attend.

_____ teacher _____ worried _____ what _____ after _____ performance. She knew _____ would _____ awful and _____. She _____ tell _____ lie, _____ she didn't _____ hurt Claire's feelings _____. Finally, she _____ idea and went backstage _____ greet _____ former pupil.

"Well," _____ Claire, "what _____ think _____ performance?"

"My dear," _____ teacher, "you'll _____ better _____ were tonight."

B. What Do You Think?

Circle the best answer to each of the following questions.

1. What was the most important thing in Claire's life?
   a) music
   b) money
   c) love

2. What did Claire's teacher finally do?
   a) she encouraged her
   b) she raised her fee for the lessons
   c) she gave up and stopped the lessons

3. What did Claire do?
   a) she quit
   b) she gave a concert
   c) she became a voice teacher

C. Learning New Words

Complete each sentence in four different ways. Indicate in the spaces provided whether each answer is True (T) or False (F).

1. If your English **IMPROVES,** you probably
   have an excellent teacher _____
   study every day _____
   are very lucky _____
   don't study at all _____

2. If you decide to **GIVE UP** studying something, you are probably
   bored _____
   having a lot of trouble in class _____
   discouraged _____
   overworked _____

3. If someone **HURTS YOUR FEELINGS,** you will probably
   feel very bad _____
   feel wonderful _____
   get angry _____
   talk about it with a good friend _____

D. Mix and Match

Complete the following sentence in four different ways. Use any vocabulary you like from lists A, B, and C.

            A   B

Sam was _____ but he _____

            _____   _____

            _____   _____

            _____   _____

                         C

and eventually he _____

                  _____

                  _____

                  _____

A	B	C
a very talented musician	broke his leg	gave it up.
a wonderful dancer	drank too much	succeeded.
an excellent writer	worked very hard	had to quit.
not very talented	didn't practice	failed.

E. Ask Your Partner

Ask your partner the following questions. Write the answers in the space provided.

		Yes	No
1.	Do you like to sing?	___	___
2.	Did you ever take music lessons when you were a child?	___	___
3.	Have you ever sung in public?	___	___
4.	Do you get nervous if you have to speak or perform in public?	___	___
5.	Would you like to be an opera star?	___	___
6.	Do you usually sing in the shower?	___	___
7.	Did your mother ever sing you to sleep when you were a child?	___	___
8.	Would you like to sing with a rock band?	___	___
9.	Can you read music?	___	___
10.	Are you a musician?	___	___

F. Put It in Writing

Write ten complete sentences about your partner, using the information you have learned in Exercise E.

Example: If your partner answered **YES** to the first question, you will write: He likes to sing.

Have You Heard This One?

WHAT DID THE BIG HAND ON THE CLOCK SAY TO
THE LITTLE HAND?

Go right ahead. I'll be back in an hour!

18 R.S.V.P.

A very boring and snobbish woman met George Bernard Shaw, the famous Irish playwright, at a garden party one afternoon in London.

She was the sort of woman who was only interested in people who were rich or famous, preferably both, and she was very eager to have Shaw as a guest in her own home so she could show him off to her friends.

One day she sent her chauffeur in a black Rolls Royce to Shaw's home with the following invitation:

*Lady Whitley-Fallwell will be at home
on Thursday, the 14th of December,
from 4 to 6*

The following reply came back immediately:

So will Mr. G.B. Shaw

A. Listen and Complete

Listen to your teacher read the story and fill in the missing words in the spaces indicated.

A very _____ and snobbish _____ met George Bernard Shaw, _____ English playwright, at _____ garden party _____ afternoon _____ London.

She _____ sort _____ woman _____ only interested _____ people _____ rich _____ famous, preferably _____, and _____ very eager _____ Shaw _____ guest _____ home _____ she _____ show _____ off _____ friends.

_____ day she _____ chauffeur _____ black Rolls Royce _____ Shaw's home _____ following invitation:

Lady Whitley-Fallwell _____ at _____

_____ Thursday, _____ 14th

_____ December,

_____ 4 _____ 6

_____ following reply _____ immediately:

_____ Mr. G.B. Shaw

B. What Do You Think?

Circle the best answer to each of the following questions.

1. What sort of woman was Lady Whitley-Fallwell?
   - a) an ordinary woman
   - b) an interesting woman
   - c) a snobbish woman

2. Why did she decide to invite G.B. Shaw to her home?
   - a) she thought he was lonely
   - b) she wanted to lend him some money
   - c) she wanted to show him off to her friends

3. How did she send the invitation?
   - a) she mailed it
   - b) she dropped it off in person
   - c) she sent it with her chauffeur

C. Learning New Words

Complete each sentence in four different ways. Indicate in the spaces provided whether each answer is True (T) or False (F).

1. If a person is **SNOBBISH,** he probably
   - has lots of friends _____
   - doesn't have many friends _____
   - loves expensive things _____
   - doesn't like cheap things _____

2. If you go to a **BORING** movie, you'll probably
   - want to see it again _____
   - want to leave before it's over _____
   - tell all your friends to see it _____
   - wish you hadn't gone _____

3. If a person is eager to **SHOW OFF** his new apartment, he is probably
   - proud of it _____
   - pleased with it _____
   - ashamed of it _____
   - thrilled over it _____

D. Mix and Match

Complete the following sentence in four different ways. Use any vocabulary you like from lists A, B, and C.

A	B

He wasn't a very _____ but he always had _____

_____   _____

_____   _____

_____   _____

C

because he had _____

_____

_____

_____

A	B	C
experienced teacher	lots of patients	a swimming pool.
friendly doctor	lots of students	a very good mind.
interesting man	lots of	an excellent
handsome man	girlfriends	reputation.
	lots of house	a wonderful
	guests	personality.

E. Ask Your Partner

Ask your partner the following questions. Write the answers in the space provided.

		Yes	No
1.	Do you think that money brings happiness?	_____	_____
2.	Do you spend money easily?	_____	_____
3.	Have you ever borrowed money from a friend?	_____	_____
4.	Do you think it is possible to be good friends with a person who is much wealthier than you are?	_____	_____
5.	Do you believe that "Money is the root of all evil"?	_____	_____
6.	Have you ever met a person who name dropped?	_____	_____
7.	Have you ever asked anyone for an autograph?	_____	_____
8.	Has anyone ever asked you for your autograph?	_____	_____
9.	Would you like to marry a famous person?	_____	_____
10.	Have you ever ridden in a Rolls Royce?	_____	_____

F. Put It in Writing

Write ten complete sentences about your partner, using the information you have learned in Exercise E.

> **Example:** If your partner answered **YES** to the first question, you will write:
> He thinks that money brings happiness.

Have You Heard This One?

WHAT DID THE BIG ENVELOPE SAY TO
THE LITTLE STAMP?

Stick with me and we'll go places!

19 The Bear

One day a black bear met a man in the forest. The bear was big. The man was small. The bear was fat. The man was skinny. The bear had beautiful, shiny, soft black hair. The man was bald.

They began to fight. The man had a gun and the bear didn't, but in spite of this obvious disadvantage, the bear won.

After the fight, the big black bear was telling the story to a friend. "You know," he said, "I just had a fight with a man with a gun and guess what? I won!"

"I know," said his friend. "I was watching the fight, and it's a shame."

"What do you mean?" asked the bear.

"Well," said his friend, "he's going to make a very ugly rug."

A. Listen and Complete

Listen to your teacher read the story and fill in the missing words in the spaces indicated.

_____ day _____ black bear

_____ man _____ forest.

_____ bear _____ big.

_____ man _____ small.

_____ bear _____ fat.

_____ man _____ skinny.

_____ bear _____ beautiful, shiny,

_____ black hair. _____ man

_____ bald.

They _____ fight. _____ man

_____ gun _____ bear

_____, but _____ this obvious

disadvantage, _____ bear _____.

After _____ fight, _____ black bear

_____ the story _____ friend. "You

know," _____, "I _____ had

_____ fight _____ man

_____ gun and guess what? I _____!"

"I know," _____ friend. "I _____

watching _____ fight, and it's _____

shame."

"What _____ mean?" _____ bear.

"Well," _____ friend, "he's _____

make _____ ugly rug."

B. What Do You Think?

Circle the best answer to each of the following questions.

1. What kind of man did the big bear meet in the forest?
    - a) a fat man
    - b) a handsome man
    - c) a bald man

2. What was the man's obvious advantage?
    - a) he was stronger
    - b) he had a gun
    - c) he was bigger

3. What did the bear's friend say to him after the fight?
    - a) who won?
    - b) congratulations!
    - c) that's a shame

C. Learning New Words

Complete each sentence in four different ways. Indicate in the spaces provided whether each answer is True (T) or False (F).

1. If a person is **SKINNY,** he should
    - lose weight   _____
    - go on a diet   _____
    - gain some weight   _____
    - cut out sweets   _____

2. If a mistake is **OBVIOUS,**
    - you can't hide it   _____
    - everyone will see it   _____
    - no one will notice it   _____
    - you will know it immediately _____

3. The biggest **DISADVANTAGE** of living in a big city is
    - the high cost of living   _____
    - you can't find a good restaurant _____
    - there is nothing to do at night _____
    - the lack of privacy   _____

D. Mix and Match

Complete the following sentence in four different ways. Use any vocabulary you like from lists A, B, and C.

           A   B

The _____ met a _____ in the forest

    _____   _____

    _____   _____

    _____   _____

                                    C

but he didn't shoot him because _____

                            _____

                            _____

                            _____

A	B	C
old hunter	huge bear	he didn't know how.
young	dangerous	he didn't have a gun.
man	lion	he was too scared to
tiny man	white rabbit	shoot.
fat man	a deer	he loved animals.

E. Ask Your Partner

Ask your partner the following questions. Write the answers in the space provided.

	Yes	No
1. Do you think men are more intelligent than animals?	_____	_____
2. Do you agree that "Man's best friend is his dog"?	_____	_____
3. Have you ever seen a bear?	_____	_____
4. Have you ever gone hunting?	_____	_____
5. Do you have a fur coat?	_____	_____
6. Do you have a pet at home?	_____	_____
7. Have you ever been frightened by an animal?	_____	_____
8. Do you think cats are friendlier than dogs?	_____	_____
9. Are you fond of animals?	_____	_____
10. Are you afraid of snakes?	_____	_____

F. Put It in Writing

Write ten complete sentences about your partner, using the information you have learned in Exercise E.

Example: If your partner answered **YES** to the first question, you will write:
He thinks that men are more intelligent than animals.

Have You Heard This One?

WHAT DID THE LITTLE RUG SAY TO THE CEILING?

Stop staring at me!

20 The Bad Check

One day a middle-aged woman telephoned her doctor.

"Doctor," she said, "I'm having a lot of trouble with my shoulder. It hurts all the time and I can't sleep at night."

"Come in this afternoon," said the doctor, "and I'll have a look at it."

That afternoon the woman went to the doctor's office. He gave her a very thorough examination, asked a lot of questions, and listened carefully to her answers.

"Well, my dear," he said, "it looks like you have arthritis."

"Arthritis?" she said. "Oh, no! What am I going to do?"

"Don't worry," he answered, "I'll give you a prescription and the pain will go away." Then the doctor took out his pen, wrote a prescription, and handed her his bill for fifty dollars. The woman opened her pocketbook, wrote out a fifty-dollar check, said goodbye, and left.

The doctor mailed the check to his bank, but a week later he was surprised to find that the check was returned to him, marked "Insufficient Funds." He telephoned the woman immediately.

"I'm very sorry to have to tell you this," be began, "but your check came back this week."

"Oh really?" said the woman. "That's quite a coincidence."

"What do you mean?" asked the doctor.

"Well," said the woman, "so did my arthritis."

A.   Listen and Complete

Listen to your teacher read the story and fill in the missing words in the spaces indicated.

_____ day _____ middle-aged woman telephoned _____ doctor.

"Doctor," _____ , "I'm _____ a lot _____ trouble _____ shoulder. _____ hurts _____ time _____ can't sleep _____ night."

"Come _____ this afternoon," _____ doctor, "_____ I'll have _____ look _____ ."

_____ afternoon _____ woman went _____ doctor's office. _____ gave _____ very thorough examination, asked _____ questions, _____ listened carefully _____ answers.

"Well, _____ dear," _____ , "it looks _____ you _____ arthritis."

"Arthritis?" _____ . "Oh, no! What _____ going to _____ ?"

"Don't worry," _____ answered, "I'll give _____ prescription _____ pain _____ go away." Then _____ doctor took out _____ pen, _____ prescription, _____ handed _____ his bill _____ fifty dollars. _____ woman opened _____ pocketbook, wrote _____ fifty-dollar check, _____ goodbye, and _____ .

_____ doctor mailed _____ check _____ bank, _____ week later _____ surprised _____ find _____ check _____ returned to him, marked "Insufficient Funds." _____ telephoned _____ woman immediately.

"I'm very sorry _____ tell _____ this," _____ began, "but _____ check _____ back _____ week."

"_____ really?" _____ woman. "That's _____ coincidence."

"What _____ mean?" asked _____ doctor.

"Well," _____ woman, "_____ did _____ arthritis."

B. What Do You Think?

Circle the best answer to each of the following questions.

1. Why did the woman telephone her doctor?
   a) she wanted to know how he was feeling
   b) she was having trouble with her shoulder
   c) she was lonely and wanted to talk to someone

2. What did the doctor advise her to do?
   a) take a pain killer
   b) take a vacation
   c) get a second opinion

3. Why was the doctor surprised a week later?
   a) his patient was feeling much better
   b) his patient's check was no good
   c) his shoulder started to bother him

C. Learning New Words

Complete each sentence in four different ways. Indicate in the spaces provided whether each answer is True (T) or False (F).

1. A **THOROUGH** physical examination probably will
   take quite a long time   _____
   take a few minutes   _____
   cost a lot   _____
   include X-rays   _____

2. If your feet **HURT** you should
   soak them in hot water   _____
   drink a glass of ice tea   _____
   sit down for a while   _____
   go for a long walk   _____

3. It's quite a **COINCIDENCE** if
   you receive a phone call from a friend just at the
   moment you were going to call him   _____
   you run into someone from your home town while
   you are on vacation in a large city   _____
   you and your best friend both have the same first name   _____
   you and your sister speak the same language   _____

D. Mix and Match

Complete the following sentence in four different ways. Use any vocabulary you like from lists A, B, and C.

		A			B	
The	_____		had	_____		

The _____ had _____

_____   _____

_____   _____

_____   _____

C

so he followed his doctor's advice and _____

_____

_____

_____

A	B	C
taxi driver	swollen feet	went home and went to bed.
garbage	a terrible headache	took a hot bath.
man	a bad back	took two aspirin.
policeman	an awful cold	drank hot tea with lemon.
waiter		

E. Ask Your Partner

Ask your partner the following questions. Write the answers in the space provided.

		Yes	No
1.	Have you ever written a bad check?	_____	_____
2.	Would you accept a check from a stranger?	_____	_____
3.	Do you usually pay in cash when you visit your doctor?	_____	_____
4.	Have you ever had arthritis?	_____	_____
5.	Do doctors make house calls in your country?	_____	_____
6.	Have you ever had back trouble?	_____	_____
7.	How many times did you visit your doctor last year?	_____	
8.	How much does a regular doctor's visit cost in your country?	_____	
9.	What do you take for a headache?	_____	
10.	How are you feeling today?	_____	

F. Put It in Writing

Write ten complete sentences about your partner, using the information you have learned in Exercise E.

> **Example:** If your partner answered **NO** to the first question, you will write:
> He hasn't ever written a bad check.

Have You Heard This One?

WHAT DID ONE ELEVATOR SAY TO THE OTHER?

I think I'm coming down with something!